HUNTERS & JUMPERS

BY
NANCY ROBISON

EDITED BY
DR. HOWARD SCHROEDER
**Professor In Reading and Language Arts
Dept. of Elementary Education
Mankato State University**

DESIGNED & PRODUCED BY
BAKER STREET PRODUCTIONS
MANKATO, MINNESOTA

COVER GRAPHICS BY
BOB WILLIAMS

CRESTWOOD HOUSE
Mankato, Minnesota

CIP

LIBRARY OF CONGRESS CATALOGING IN PUBLICATION DATA

Robison, Nancy.
  Hunters & jumpers.

  (Horses, pasture to paddock)
  SUMMARY: Discusses which horses make good hunters and jumpers; what they
do; and their buying, schooling, and showing.
  1. Hunters (Horses)--Juvenile literature. 2. Show jumpers (horses)--Juvenile
literature. (1. Hunters (Horses). 2. Show jumpers (Horses). 3. Horses.) I.
Schroeder, Howard. II. Baker Street Productions. III. Title. IV. Title. V. Series.
SF293.H8R6   1983   636.1'0888   83-7832
ISBN 0-89686-227-5

International Standard Book Numbers:	Library of Congress Catalog Card Number:
Library Binding 0-89686-227-5	83-7832

PHOTOGRAPH CREDITS

Cappy Jackson: Cover, 4, 25, 26, 29
Joseph Berke: 8
Pennington Galleries: 9, 44
Mark Ahlstrom: 11, 13, 14, 15, 17A, 17B, 17C, 19, 20, 23, 32, 34, 37, 39, 42
Patti Mack: 31
Alix Coleman: 41

CRESTWOOD HOUSE

Hwy. 66 South, Box 3427
Mankato, MN 56002-3427

TABLE
OF
CONTENTS

The traditional blessing at the start of a fox hunt.

4

INTRODUCTION

Years ago, while in England, I watched a fox hunt. It was more beautiful than I ever could have imagined. Hunters in scarlet coats and black hats rode fast, shiny horses. Across green meadows they'd go, jumping hedgerows on the way. One minute they were in sight, the next, they would disappear behind trees and bushes. Seconds later they'd be back — hounds baying, and horses galloping. It was a thrilling sight, and one I'll never forget. I worried about the fox until I learned that it had been eating the farmer's crops and chickens. I worried about the horses, running so hard and fast and for such a long time. Because of this I became interested in finding out about hunter and jumper horses.

①
BLOODLINE OF
HUNTERS AND JUMPERS

The best horses for hunting and jumping are the Thoroughbreds, or those that have some Thoroughbred blood in them. Thoroughbred does not mean the same as purebred. An Arabian horse is a purebred, which means it is not mixed with other horses of different blood. A Thoroughbred horse is part Arabian and part something else. In order to know what makes a good hunter or jumper, it is necessary to know the background of the Thoroughbred horse. And the Thoroughbred's background goes back to the Arabian horse.

Thousands of years ago herds of horses roamed the land. Although most horses were wild at that time, the Arabian horse was being trained to do tricks, and it had special care.

Families that lived in Arabia loved horses. They even took them into their tents. The love and care

An old Arabian scene gives an idea of how horses and other animals were used in parades.

that was given to these horses centuries ago shows in today's Arabian horses. With a pure bloodline and proper care, the horses show great intelligence and a gentle nature.

The greatest value of the Arabian horse is in improving other breeds. The mating of the purebred Arabian with the English mare has produced the Thoroughbred horse, a horse known for its speed and endurance (ability to run a long time). Cross-breeding the Thoroughbred with another breed (like an Arabian, Saddlebred, or Quarter Horse) will often produce a good hunter or jumper.

②
DIFFERENCES BETWEEN HUNTERS AND JUMPERS

Hunters jump and chase in fields, as well as show rings. Jumpers jump only in show rings. In a show ring, jumpers are judged on how high they can jump, and on how fast they do it. Hunters, on the other hand, are judged mostly on their style in the ring.

Not all horses are hunters, and not all horses are jumpers. The training is different. But all horses of all breeds can be hunters and jumpers.

A hunter needs many cross-country workouts, or long rides in the country. This gets the hunter used to

A hunter needs cross-country workouts.

This jumper goes over a difficult water jump.

sights, sounds, and ground conditions. The cross-country practice is not so important for a jumper because they jump in a show ring. But, it helps any horse to develop sure-footedness.

In a show ring, jumpers will jump fences, gates, walls, and water troughs. The most difficult jumps for a horse are going over an obstacle, such as a fence or wall, at an angle, and jumping when coming out of a turn. All this takes a great deal of practice.

Jumping courses are designed as a test of obedience and ability. The jumper is a trained athlete and must have advanced schooling. It has to know how to adjust strides quickly. This horse must have good takeoff, and be able to fly over obstacles without touching them. The horse should be relaxed and able to move with ease while jumping.

WHAT MAKES A GOOD HUNTER AND JUMPER?

A good hunter and jumper must be a sound horse (one without blemish or injury), and be willing to learn. Physical qualities that help make a good jumper are strong hind quarters, sound feet and legs, good sloping shoulders, good heart and wind, and a short back. Other qualities needed are natural balance and natural impulsion (a driving forward with sudden force). A natural bending of the knees and a round back when clearing an obstacle are helpful too. A natural instinct to jump clean and with courage is most important.

The horse must practice. If a horse doesn't know what it's doing, it may hurt itself and its rider. So a horse must be intelligent as well as an athlete.

BUYING A HUNTER AND JUMPER

Before buying a hunter or jumper, it is a good idea to ride the horse. This is the time to see if horse and rider can work well together.

Check the horses legs, making sure they are straight and not turned in or turned out. Look for a horse with a good disposition, or nature — one that is not easily excited or nervous. Make sure it is a sound horse, free from injury or defects. And, of course, the horse must have jumping ability. Conformation (the appearance) of the horse is not as important as the bloodlines. A good hunter or jumper should have at least three-fourths to seven-eighths Thoroughbred blood in it.

Check the horse's legs carefully before buying it to make sure they are straight.

③
SCHOOLING

No horse should be taught to jump without basic schooling first. The horse should start with long exercise periods and work up to jumping. Learning to jump usually starts when the horse is four years old.

The first thing to do is find a place to practice, like a corral or fenced-in area. First practice walking the horse. Walk in both directions around the enclosed area. Then trot your horse in both directions. Then canter. Repeat this drill over and over again — walk, trot, canter. Then do it with a loose rein, holding on with control, but not too tightly. While you practice, talk to your horse and give it encouragement.

TIPS TO REMEMBER

During schooling you will be around your horse quite a lot. It is important to know how to act around a horse. Always make slow movements or you may scare the horse. Never stand where it can kick you. It's better to stand by the head, where the horse can see you, than behind it. Do not walk under its neck while it is tied because the horse might jerk its neck back against the rope. Generally try to handle a horse from its near, or left, side. If you pet the horse, do it on the neck, under the chin or on the withers (shoulders). Never reach for its nose or ears, which are the most sensitive parts of a horse. Horses do not like to be touched there. Horses learn by memory — by doing things over and over again. Be patient while teaching your horse.

It's best to handle a horse from the near, or left, side.

PREPARING TO JUMP

Most horses can jump small obstacles like ditches and things that are low to the ground. But horses need to go to school to learn how to jump safely with a rider on their back. The first jumping lessons are done with just the horse. There is no rider on its back.

The horse is led over a pole on the ground, not jumping or leaping, but in its stride. That is, the horse should just step over the pole. This is done while keeping the horse calm and quiet. It should become a normal activity, like when a person walks up or down stairs. The horse is being trained men-

A horse is led over poles on the ground as one of the first steps in training.

Using a longe line, a trainer guides the horse over a low jump.

tally as well as physically. It is learning to concentrate as well as to perform. The horse must be able to take instructions.

One way to work a horse is on a longe line. This is a very long rein. The trainer can guide the horse around in a circle by this line. The horse should work in both directions — right and left. A long whip flicked on the ground will encourage the horse to keep moving.

The next step could be working over a low jump. To start with, one pole is low to the ground and fixed with only one side up, maybe three inches off the ground. Then with two poles crossed in the middle forming an X. The horse can learn to cross over in the middle where the X forms and it is lowest to the ground. The poles can be raised to make higher jumps when the horse is ready. Most riders work up slowly to a three-foot jump.

The most important thing about training is that a horse learn to jump the right way. From the very beginning, a horse should learn to use its feet correctly. The horse has to learn to be "collected," (to keep its feet under itself when getting ready to jump), because it isn't natural. The horse also has to learn to carry most of its weight on its rear legs. Its spine must arc or curve when it goes over a jump.

Training fences should be solid and heavy, not light. When a horse doesn't lift and hits a solid pole, it will learn to lift the next time. Bandages around the horses legs will help protect them from bruises. A horse will enjoy jumping if it does not get hurt or frightened. However, a horse should not be made to jump higher than it is ready to jump.

When a horse can jump a three foot high fence with ease by itself, the rider can then mount. Once the rider is on the horses back, the lessons start all over again. First the rider will walk the horse over a pole on the ground, then trot it over, and then canter. Once a horse is comfortable doing this, a series of six poles can be put down, spaced a stride apart. The horse will walk over them naturally. Then the horse is trotted and cantered over the poles. Finally the poles are raised and the horse learns to jump a series of obstacles.

Training takes time and patience. It is not done in one day, but a little bit every day over and over again.

After mounting, the rider takes the horse over a series of poles at a walk (top), trot (center), and canter (bottom).

READY FOR THE JUMP

Before even taking a horse to a jump, the rider should study the jump. The rider must know the jump before he or she can expect the horse to know.

The uprights at each end of the jump are called posts. The poles between these posts are called bars. The bars can be raised or lowered to the height the horse will be able to jump. There should always be at least two bars. One of them is kept at ground level to help the horse judge the height of the jump. To begin, the rider will remove both bars and put them on the ground between the posts. The rider is now ready to walk the horse between the posts and over the bars. But first, he or she must make one last check on the horse's equipment, making sure the saddle and bridle are on right. The rider mounts slowly, takes the reins in both hands and guides the horse between the two posts and over the middle of the bars. After going in one direction for a while, the rider will turn around and go through the posts the other way. This gets the horse used to the jump.

The rider must always let the horse know when it is doing well. A gentle pat on the neck and a soft word of praise will help keep the horse calm.

The next step is to slowly trot the horse through the posts. A slow trot is done like the walk. The horse just goes straight through the middle of the jump a little faster than the walk. At this time, the rider can

This rider walks her horse through the jump.

begin to lift slightly off the saddle. This "two-point position" gives the rider and horse a feel of lifting for a jump. The rider should always look between the horse's ears, not down at the bars. Finally, the horse will canter through the posts and over the bars.

When the horse is ready to jump, the rider will first take it over a low bar. Then one bar will be gradually raised to three feet. Even if a horse is doing well, it is not a good idea to rush the training. Learning to jump is a slow process.

When teaching a horse to jump higher than three feet or a series of jumps, some trainers go back to the

Some trainers make a low jump by crossing two bars.

longe line. Again, working slowly with the horse before it learns to jump with a rider.

CONDITIONING

Just as you and I like to run barefoot now and then, so do horses. Once a year in warm weather, horses are turned out unshod (without shoes) in green pastures to run freely. This comes after they work hard all year.

After a rest, it's time to get back to work. But, the horse will need "conditioning." That is, it will have to be worked to get muscles and wind built up again. Walking up and down hills is good conditioning. Hunter and jumper horses like to run along wet sandy beaches. The salt water makes a good leg bath.

A horse may cut back on its eating during its rest period. But during this conditioning time a horse may need to have more food then it did in its rest period.

An expert trainer will know when a horse is ready to go back to work.

An interesting story is told about a Thoroughbred race horse named Rubio. In 1908, when Rubio showed signs of getting tired, its owners shipped the horse to England. There, the horse got a job pulling a bus. After three years, someone noticed that Rubio liked to jump. The horse was put back into training and conditioning. After the conditioning program, Rubio was entered in the Grand National of the Steeplechase Race. Only the best horses are entered in this race. Guess who won? Rubio did, by ten full lengths.

This story shows two things. First, maybe Rubio needed a rest from racing, and secondly maybe pulling the bus helped build new muscles for jumping. But whatever it was, the conditioning program helped Rubio become a winner.

ACCIDENTS AND FALLS

A crash helmet, or hard hat, is a good thing to wear while training a horse to jump. As serious as a fall may look for the horse, it can hurt the rider more than the horse. Horses may take a spill, but most of the time they'll get right back up again.

When a horse falls, it is important to keep calm. Help it up by holding the reins. Then when the horse gets up, walk it around. Check for wounds or bruises. Make sure the horse is all right before riding it again. If any treatment is needed, take the horse back to the stables immediately.

Hunters and jumpers can take bad spills. Sometimes a bone gets broken, but this does not mean the horse must be destroyed. Horses have recovered from breaks and gone on to run again.

PONIES MAKE
GOOD JUMPERS

Some ponies make good jumpers. The Connemara and Welsh ponies take to it easily. In fact, any

Both ponies and horses will sometimes "refuse" a jump.

pony that is strong and wants to jump can be taught.

Ponies are trained just like big horses. But because they are short, ponies have to be trained not to hop over a jump, they have to learn to stride over it.

Sometimes ponies will "refuse" a jump. They like to run around the jump instead of going over. They can learn to jump, though, just like a big horse.

Pony hunts for young people are sponsored by pony clubs around the country. The pony hunt is designed to train riders for fox hunting. (See Chapter Four).

④
WHAT HUNTERS DO

A hunter does not jump like an open jumper. A jumper clears high fences. The hunter will meet many different types of obstacles during a long day's hunt. It would tire if all the jumps were big ones, so some shorter jumps are used, too.

Hunter horses perform in horse shows. They also run in a race called Steeplechase and are used for fox hunting. A horse that likes to go on a chase makes a good hunter horse.

THE FOX HUNT

A fox hunt is really a chase. Hounds do the hunting. The horses and riders just follow.

Long ago, the Egyptians, Persians, Greeks, Romans, and early Britons used horses to chase wild animals for food. This chase soon turned into a sport. Fox hunting was done for the joy of riding a good horse across the countryside and to watch hounds at work.

The sport of fox hunting began in England around 1690. Farmers wanted to rid their gardens of fox, deer, and rabbit. The sport was brought to America sixty years later. George Washington had a pack of hounds and enjoyed the sport. Today, the hunt is not

24

always after a fox. Some hunts go after coyotes or other vermin (small animals that are destructive).

There also is a chase called a "drag" hunt. This is done when there is no fox around. A make-believe hunt is put together by having someone drag a burlap bag with fox scent on it. The hounds will follow the scent, and the chase is on!

A rider waits for the hounds to pick up the fox scent.

RULES FOR FOX HUNTS

There are a few rules a rider should know before going on a fox hunt. The master of the fox hounds takes the lead and riders must stay behind the master at all times. The most important part of the hunt is the hounds. Riders do not talk when the hounds are working and they must keep out of the way of the hounds. Riders never turn their backs on the hounds. To get out of the way, horses must be backed up. Riders must never jump a fence if hounds are in the way and never get between the hounds and the master. Riders should never jump a fence until the hounds have cleared it first.

Fox hunting takes riders across many different parts of the countryside.

In a hunt, the senior (more experienced) members always go first. A horse approaching a fence straight on goes over first. Those on an angle wait until the way is clear. If a horse refuses to jump a fence or brush, it must be gotten out of the way for the others.

Riders always follow the master. They do not damage the land, and they must go around plowed areas and herds of cattle or sheep. A rider doesn't gallop past a fallen horse and rider, but stops to help. A horse should be in good condition at the finish of the hunt. If a horse gets tired, lame, or unruly, it is taken home. At the end of the day, the rider thanks the master for the hunt.

At home, the rider makes sure the horse is cooled down, well-fed, clean, and comfortable. The horse must be checked for any scratches or cuts and then groomed. The next morning, the horse should be taken for a little walk, and given a day of rest.

CLOTHING FOR A FOX HUNT

Part of the tradition that goes with a fox hunt is the clothing. In bygone times in England, when the king owned all the game, anyone going on the hunt had to wear the king's color. This was red. The idea stuck and today most riders wear scarlet, a shade of red, coats. But some prefer blue, brown, black, or gray tweed riding coats. Tall black boots are usually worn, as are white shirts and black ties. A hard hat made of velvet, a hunting cap, or riding derby is worn. String gloves sometimes are worn too.

THE STEEPLECHASE RACE

The Steeplechase race started in England long ago. Horse riders would race on weekends from a farm to a church steeple. On the way they jumped fences, hedges, and stone walls at full speed. Steeple-chasing soon became as popular as regular horse racing. It's an exciting and thrilling race, but it is exhausting and dangerous, too. More skill and courage is needed by horse and rider in the Steeplechase than in any other race. Horses have to be specially trained.

In regular races, usually all horses will finish. This is not always so in the Steeplechase. In this race, many things can happen. Horses often fall on top of one another while jumping fences (fences are obstacles like rails, brush, stone walls, white boards, gates, chicken coops and hedges). If they are not hurt, they can be remounted and the race goes on. Some horses have been known to win even after falling many times. Because this is a rugged race, straps might break causing the saddle to slip off. Yet, jockeys

In Steeplechase racing the horses must have strong legs for jumping and running.

have gone on to finish the race bareback. Should the lead horse fall, other horses racing right behind it may pile on top. In each case, not all horses will finish the race.

For Steeplechasing, horses must have strong legs and powerful thighs since there are many obstacles to jump. The horse lands on one foot, with the others following immediately, so they need heavy leg bones too. Well-developed shoulders are needed for cushioning the landing. Horses used for steeplechasing must have good reflexes to dodge a fallen horse or other obstacle.

POINT-TO-POINT RACE

The Point-to-Point race is much like the Steeplechase. It is found wherever fox hunting is enjoyed. The course is marked with flags over five miles of countryside. The point-to-point race is much like a fox hunt without hounds or a fox. It usually is done after the fox hunting season is over. No one under the age of eighteen can enter this race because it is difficult and dangerous. In this race, horses must jump all types of barriers. A hunter horse is used for this race, and it must be a good one — usually a Thoroughbred. Besides riding over the countryside for hours, the horse must jump walls, fences and waterways. The horse has to be an intelligent and obedient animal and be able to go, stop, and stand without becoming impatient.

⑤
WHAT JUMPERS DO

Jumpers are entered in horse shows, where they jump over man-made "fences." These shows are fun to watch as well as fun for every horse owner to show off his or her horse. But more than this, horse shows encourage better breeds of horses. However, it is an expensive hobby. Prize money does not cover the cost of feeding, boarding or training a horse for its many years. Some big-time shows can offer large amounts of prize money, but not everyone can be a winner, of course.

This jumper goes over a man-made "fence."

There are plenty of smaller shows where the horse lover can have fun showing off his or her horse. Any horse is more valuable for resale after winning a few blue ribbons.

The horse gets a ribbon, and the rider receives a trophy, for winning an event.

Horse shows are fun and healthy events. They teach self-discipline, good sportsmanship and how to be both a graceful loser and a good winner. Winners' ribbons are pinned to the bridle of the horse and a trophy goes to the first place winner.

ENTERING A JUMPING CONTEST

If you are thinking of entering your horse in a jumping contest, make sure you are ready for it. Otherwise, it may be bad for your horse and you. First, you must take lessons and practice for several years. If you are going to jump your horse, you should build a few jumps like the ones used in a show. At least four jumps should be made. A "brush" jump with white rails and green brush around it would be a good one to make. This is a difficult jump, and one that a horse often refuses to jump over. A natural "post and rail" jump, and a "chicken coop" made with imitation stone on one side and a sloping board wall on the other are common. A plain white "gate" could be the fourth jump. If there is a riding stable nearby with jumps already set up, this is an ideal place to learn and practice.

Jumping lessons are very important. Sometimes a jumping chute or "Hitchcock pen" is used for training a jumper. A chute is an enclosed lane with high walls and moveable obstacles. The horse is let loose in the chute without a rider so it can jump in complete freedom. This helps the animal develop good form.

The correct way to jump a horse is for the rider to lean forward with his or her seat off the saddle. This is called the "two-point position." The rider stays in this position until the horse takes a stride or two after landing. Jumps should be taken straight on, not at an angle. The rider makes a wide circle and jumps across the middle of the obstacle. The rider should not be frightened because the horse will sense it. There is an old saying, "throw your heart over the

This rider practices the "two-point" position while going over a fence.

fence," which means to mentally jump over.

When the horse extends its neck and head to get over the jump, the rider lets his or her arms extend with it. The rider always leans forward so as not to be bounced off.

Much patience is needed to train the horse. There is no short cut. The average age of a top jumper is twelve to thirteen years.

DIVISIONS FOR HUNTERS

Hunters can also be shown at horse shows. In the hunter division, there are three classes: Breeding, Conformation and Working Hunter. In the Breeding class the owner shows the horse in hand. That is, he or she will lead the horse into the ring where it will be judged on its appearance only. Conformation classes are shown under saddle. Both appearance and performance are scored. The Working Hunter class horse is judged on soundness, performance over a jumping course, and winning of the race.

Each of these three classes has two divisions. The Green Hunter class for beginning horses has lower fences than the Regular Hunter class. Fences for the Green Hunter are forty-two to forty-five inches (108-115 cm) high. A Regular Hunter jumps fences that are forty-five to fifty-four inches (115-138 cm).

TERMS TO KNOW FOR HORSE SHOWS

Horses that have not won a blue ribbon are called "maiden." One that has not yet won three blue ribbons is a "novice." And a horse that has not yet won six blue ribbons is called a "limit."

A Green Hunter horse is one of any age in its first or second year of showing over lower jumps. The Handy Hunter is an advanced horse that jumps fences at an angle. It can also make sharp turns on a twisty course.

The Puissance Jumper goes over high jumps and is always exciting to watch. These are the highest and most difficult jumps. Winners of this event have cleared a seven foot wall. This is a race of speed, strength and accuracy. Horses of this race need careful training. Racing from one fence to another at break neck speed takes timing. The horse for this race must be able to move quickly and with ease. It also must be obedient. The rider has to have good control of the horse at all times.

GROOMING

Many horses have full manes and tails. When showing, hunters and jumpers usually have braided manes and tails. Sometimes the ends of the braids are fastened with yarn or thread of the same color as the hunter's coat.

When a horse's mane is braided, its tail also is braided. On rainy days, it's tail might be braided into a "mud tail," or tight braid tucked up to make a small stub.

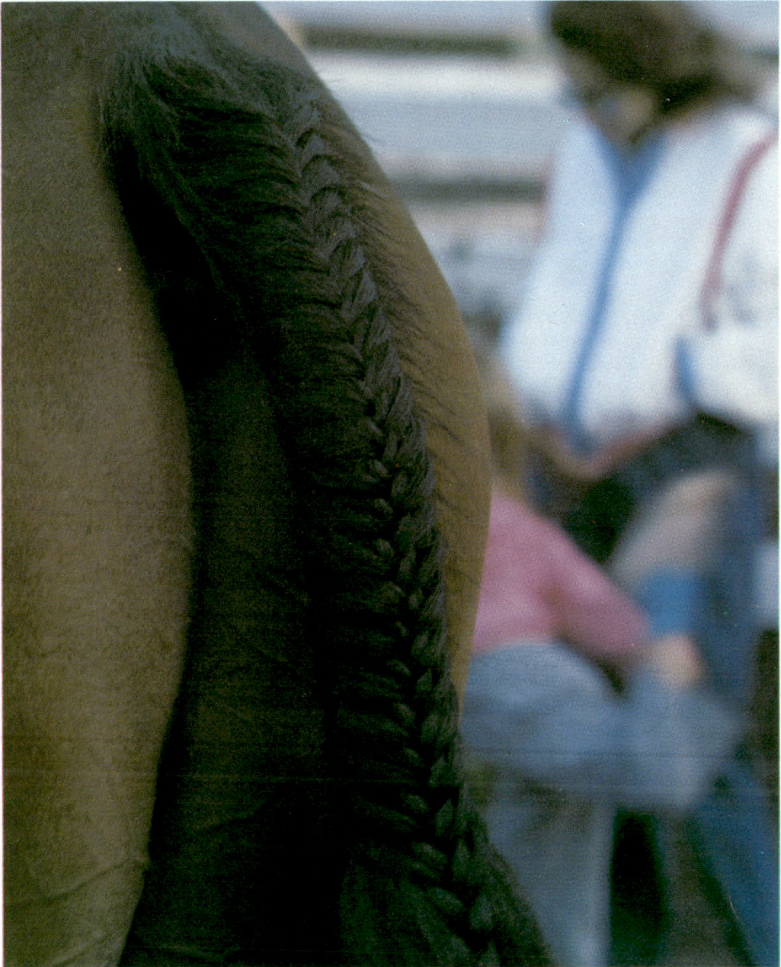

This horse's tail has been tightly braided for a show.

Washing, cleaning, brushing, clipping, combing, and grooming the mane and tail all take time, but it shows a well-kept horse.

To brighten a white coat, white rice powder can be rubbed into the damp hair of the horse and brushed away before the show. Cornstarch can be rubbed into a dry coat.

Black liquid hoof polish is used to shine up dark hoofs.

JUDGING
HUNTERS AND JUMPERS

Judging is an art. Judges watch a horse carefully. Horses are not always judged for the best looks. Sometimes they are judged only on their performance.

The rider can help the horse by knowing its strong and weak points. Therefore, it is important for rider and horse to work together. It is not a good idea to overjump a horse before a show. Training should be done well ahead of time. Two days before the competition, the horse can be taken over a few jumps. The day before, the horse should be allowed to relax and be calm. To win at show jumping, both horse and rider should be calm and confident.

A hunter judge is mainly looking for one quality in

Polish is often put on a horse's hoofs before a show.

a hunter — a sound horse that will carry a rider safely across the countryside. The hunter judge watches the horse from the minute it gets into the ring. The judge watches how the horse crosses corners. Does it make clean jumps? Does it make a clean landing or a sloppy one? Sometimes the judge will ride the horse to test it.

WHAT MAKES A GOOD SHOW JUMPER?

The way a horse looks has nothing to do with it being a good jumper. Some beautiful horses cannot jump. Some jumpers look like they belong pulling a plow, but they can "jet" over obstacles. The show jumper is an athlete, a horse with talent for jumping. A show jumper must have courage and be a relaxed horse because there is a lot of stress put on a show jumper. Besides the high jumps it must make when competing, it also must travel a lot to different shows. This can make a horse nervous.

Training a show jumper takes patience and courage. A show jumper is not ready for advanced training until it has completed all the basic jumps. If training is done right, the horse will develop discipline and obedience, and it will want to jump well. A horse can start training at age five and be ready to

compete at age six to seven. But few horses compete
in big shows before the age of ten.

Jumpers usually have to go over higher jumps in a show ring than hunters.

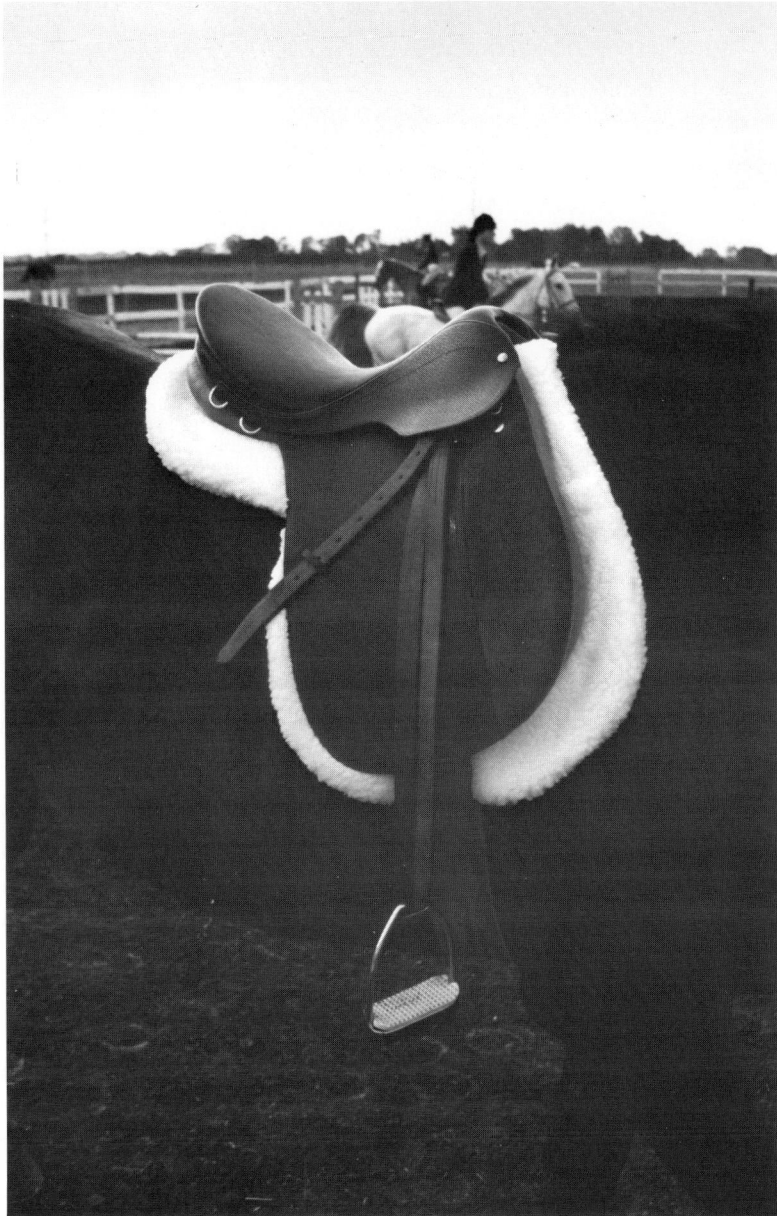

A pad is used under the forward seat saddle that is used for hunting and jumping.

EQUIPMENT

For hunting and jumping a forward seat saddle is used. The forward seat, or jumping saddle, allow's the rider's body weight to be over the horse's center of balance. The rider sits forward using a shortened stirrup. From this position it is easier for the horse to jump. The horse is allowed complete freedom to stretch out its head and neck, and to arc over a fence.

A saddle protects the horse's back. It also allows the rider to shift weight when the horse's balance changes or when it stops and jumps. A saddle is made so it won't touch a horse's spine. Pads are used under heavy saddles to protect the leather from dirt and hair.

Ladies sometimes ride on hunts in sidesaddle. The sidesaddle has a flat seat with only one stirrup. Both legs of the rider are on the same side of the horse. However, forward seat saddle is the most popular of all, because it enables the rider to go with the horse.

A hunter rider sits down when galloping a horse in a show ring. But when riding in the field on a hunt, the rider will raise up putting the body weight over his or her feet in the stirrups. If a rider were to sit all the time, the horse would get tired.

Some ladies ride in a sidesaddle to jump.

INTERNATIONAL EVENTS

International jumping is done with teams. Jumping teams from Canada, Mexico, England, Germany, South America, Spain, France, and the United States all participate in these events. It is fun to watch as horses fly over obstacles.

Every four years, the Olympic games are held in some city in the world. In 1984, they will be in Los Angeles, California, and people from all over will attend. Some of them will want to watch the four

Olympic equestrian (horse) events on the last three days of the games.

The first event is the Grand Dressage. Dressage, in French, means "training." Dressage is a test of training in obedience and behavior. On the second day, the horse and rider will go through a Steeplechase race and cross-country endurance test. On the third day there are jumping contests.

THE PAN AMERICAN GAMES

The Pan American games are held every four years, but not the same year as the Olympics. They usually are held in the homeland of the current title holder. For instance, if the last winner was from Brazil, the next games are held there.

Whether it's at the Olympics, or just at a local riding school, hunters and jumpers are exciting to watch. They provide endless hours of fun for their riders, as well.

GLOSSARY

BAYING - To bark or howl in long, deep tones.

BREEDERS - People who handle the mating of horses to carry on a bloodline of Champions.

CONFORMATION - The shape or outline of a horse.

FENCE - Obstacles that hunters and jumpers go over.

GAIT - The different movements or speeds of a horse — like trot, pace, and walk.

GIRTH - A band put around the belly of a horse for holding on a saddle.

HAND - The measurement used to measure the height of a horse from the ground to its withers — one hand equals four inches (1.5 cm).

HOCK - The joint bending backwards in the hind leg of a horse.

HUNTER - A horse trained to be used for fox hunting and the Steeplechase Race.

IMPULSION - A force driving forward — to push or thrust.

JUMPER - A horse trained for jumping at horse shows.

MASTER OF THE FOX HOUNDS (or MFH) - The person in charge of a fox hunt and the hounds. Riders must do as the MFH says.

PACE - A two beat gait where the left front and rear feet move together, and the right front and rear feet move together.

PUREBRED - A horse whose ancestors have been registered and recognized as a breed for many generations.

STRIDE - To walk with long steps.

SUPPLE - Able to bend and move easily.

TACK - A term used for riding equipment, like the saddle, bridle, and harness.

THOROUGHBRED - A type of horse developed by breeding English mares with Arabian stallions.

TROT - A medium speed, two-beat gait where a front foot and an opposite rear foot strike the ground together.

WALK - A flat-footed, four-beat gait.

WITHERS - The highest point on the shoulder of a horse.

THE HORSES
PASTURE TO PADDOCK

**READ & ENJOY
THE ENTIRE SERIES:**

CRESTWOOD HOUSE